EFFE(

LEADERSHIP

ROBERT HELLER

DK PUBLISHING, INC.

658.4092
H477f

⊕01/35Y

A DK PUBLISHING BOOK

www.dk.com

Produced for Dorling Kindersley
by Cooling Brown

Editor Amanda Lebentz
Designer Elly King
Creative Director Arthur Brown

DTP Designer Jason Little
Production Controller Silvia La Greca

Editor Adèle Hayward
Art Editor Tassy King
US Editor Chuck Wills
Managing Editors Stephanie Jackson, Jonathan Metcalf
Managing Art Editor Nigel Duffield

First American Edition, 1999
6 8 10 9 7

Published in the United States by
DK Publishing, Inc.
375 Hudson Street New York, NY 10014

Library of Congress Cataloging-in-Publication Data

Heller, Robert, 1932-
    Effective leadership / by Robert Heller -- 1st American ed.
    p.   cm. -- (Essential managers)
    Includes index.
    ISBN 0-7894-4862-9 (alk.paper)
    1. Leadership. 2. Management. I. Title. II. Series.
HD57.7.H438 1999
658.4'092--dc21   99-15780
                                                                  CIP

Reproduced by Colourscan, Singapore
Printed in China by Wing King Tong

CONTENTS

INSPIRING
EXCELLENCE

IMPROVING YOUR
EFFECTIVENESS

INTRODUCTION

The key to truly effective leadership lies in mastering a wide range of skills, from implementing and administrating processes to inspiring others to achieve excellence. Effective Leadership shows you how to make the most of opportunities to learn to lead, whether by observing others, through formal training, or through careful evaluation of practical experience. It provides a thorough grounding in the essential skills, and shows you how to put them into action in a variety of situations. With invaluable information on the key leadership skills, including communication, coaching, using authority, learning to delegate, and developing individuals and teams, as well as 101 practical tips, this book helps you to become an inspirational and confident leader, capable of heading an effective team. Two self-assessment exercises help you to assess and improve your leadership ability.

LEARNING TO LEAD

Excellent leaders are made as well as born. To be the best, learn the essential skills of leadership through formal training courses and on-the-job experience.

FOCUSING ON QUALITY

The aim of leadership is to help others to achieve their personal best. This involves setting high but realistic performance goals for yourself and your staff, finding ways to improve operations and procedures, and striving for total quality in all areas.

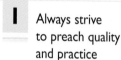

1 Always strive to preach quality and practice improvement.

APPLYING STANDARDS ▼

Work closely with subordinates to set measurable quality standards that they can seek to achieve or exceed.

SETTING STANDARDS

Before you or your staff can achieve quality goals, you need to be very clear about your own expectations regarding how things should be done and the standards of performance that must be reached. Once you have defined these expectations you can communicate them clearly to staff, emphasizing your own commitment and the fact that achieving excellence is everyone's responsibility.

Leader discusses possible areas for improvement in standards of work

Raising Standards

2 Ensure that you involve all staff members in quality-improving programs.

Maintaining and exceeding standards is an on-going process involving everyone. Encourage staff to analyze problem areas and to work together to find solutions. Involve them in looking for ways to improve products, processes, and performance, and, if extra skills are needed, arrange the necessary training. This approach not only generates ideas and innovation, but creates an atmosphere of participation and increased motivation, which in turn results in raised quality standards.

Improving Standards of Quality

Target Standards	How to Achieve Quality
Leadership Lead your team toward total quality by constantly improving every process and product.	● Ensure that all staff drive toward continuous improvement on all aspects of performance. ● Recognize and appreciate individuals and teams for the success of their efforts.
Strategy Seek to uphold and develop the organization's vision, mission, values, and direction.	● Determine all objectives with the aim of reaching the highest quality standards. ● Communicate strategic aims clearly to everybody, and review and update them regularly.
People Ensure that staff are motivated, well-managed, and empowered to improve continuously.	● Train all staff in the skills and capabilities they need to meet their quality targets. ● Practice two-way communication, top-down and bottom-up, through all available media.
Resources Aim to use financial and other resources efficiently to achieve the organization's objectives.	● Ensure money is managed efficiently and everyone understands what is happening financially and why. ● Use the best technology available and consistently update it to state-of-the-art levels.
Processes Ensure that all vital processes, including management, are consistently highly effective.	● Develop performance measures and feedback to maintain the improvement momentum. ● Stimulate people to formulate innovative and creative ideas for improving processes.

LEARNING FROM OTHERS

Every successful singer has a singing coach, and top singers often give master classes. The principle is just the same for leaders. You learn better leadership skills by being coached, and you develop those skills further by coaching others.

> **3** Always be on the lookout for chances to learn valuable lessons.

IMPROVING SKILLS

Leaders must continually assess their performance and look for ways to improve and extend their skills. A great deal can be learned by simply observing others whose behavior appears to get results. A mentor will provide informal guidance where needed, or you may choose a more formal avenue of learning, such as a training program.

> **4** Take a refresher course if you feel you need to brush up on rusty skills.

USING FORMAL TRAINING

Even leaders with years of on-the-job experience can benefit from some formal training from time to time. Outside training gives you an opportunity to get away from day-to-day activities, and provides a fresh perspective. Use training to keep abreast of current trends and to brush up on or acquire specific skills. Do not wait to be asked – assess your strengths and weaknesses and put yourself forward for courses that match your needs.

Personnel director explains new trends

Leader gains an insight into how trends may affect the organization

◀ **WIDENING KNOWLEDGE**
Take advantage of colleagues' expertise in specific areas to broaden your own skills. You can learn a great deal from people with an in-depth knowledge of their field.

COACHING OTHERS

Training others provides a valuable source of education in the skills needed to become an effective leader, such as communicating clearly, giving instructions, getting feedback, delegating, motivating, and developing people. Always ask for feedback from those you are coaching – they can provide useful insights into your own performance. Share your experience and expertise with other people to help you to clarify your own attitudes, beliefs, and priorities, and to analyze your own performance. Use any time spent coaching your staff to discover their needs, what motivates them, and how they respond to your leadership style. Develop skills in other people to enable you to delegate some of your tasks, leaving more time available for you to spend on activities that will improve your own skills as a leader.

5 Use coaching sessions to learn as well as teach.

6 Set an example to your staff by being trained yourself.

▼ **RAISING STANDARDS**
Learn new skills, develop existing ones, and use your knowledge and experience to benefit colleagues. In this way, you will improve all-around performance.

Learn ▶ Coach ▶ Raise performance

**BEING A ▶
GOOD COACH**
Taking over the task that he had assigned to Jean seemed the easy option to Gordon. But he learned from this experience that he had avoided the important issue. He was looking at the problem in the short term, rather than focusing on helping Jean to improve her skills and perform better in future. He realized that training people was far more productive than doing everything himself.

CASE STUDY
Gordon asked Jean, one of his second-level managers, to produce a report that involved a degree of financial knowledge. He took it for granted that she understood the basics of management accounting, and was unpleasantly surprised to find that Jean had made many errors through ignorance. Since time was pressing, and since this was work that came easily to him, Gordon rewrote the report and passed it on. Jean asked for an interview. She was angry, and Gordon assumed that this was because he had taken over writing the report. But Jean was cross for a different reason. As she said, "How do you expect me to learn if you don't tell me what I've done wrong?" Gordon realized that he had failed Jean. He set aside time to coach her in management accounting, and also sent her on a course in finance.

GAINING EXPERIENCE

P romotion to leadership positions used to depend on rising up the company hierarchy. Now, vital work is increasingly carried out by temporary teams working on specific projects, which provide ideal opportunities for learning leadership skills.

7 Use projects as a way of learning more about other disciplines.

JOINING PROJECT TEAMS

Widen your knowledge and learn new skills by joining a project team. These are usually set up to work on new projects within an existing organization. Such teams can become permanent if the project takes off, and are independent of the vertical hierarchy. The longer the project lasts, the more likely it is that team membership and roles will change during the project's life. This means you can join a project in a subordinate position, but with the hope of finding a leadership role later. The larger the team, and the wider its responsibilities, the greater the chance to change roles or be promoted within the team. Gaining experience on projects led by other people is also an invaluable education in leading your own project.

Subordinate is promoted to lead own team

Subordinate gains experience in leadership skills working as part of a team.

◀ LEARNING SKILLS ON PROJECT TEAMS

Working on a project team can provide you with all the necessary experience to run your own team. Show your initiative and make the most of any opportunities that arise.

LEARNING FLEXIBILITY

The leadership of a project is often passed to different people at different stages. For example, it could move from the design department to the production staff to the marketing people, each passing on the baton in turn. This gives you the opportunity to learn crucial lessons in how to organize and collaborate with different functions and departments, from finance to sales, engineering to purchasing. Although the baton changes hands, everyone still works as part of a harmonious team at all times. The abilities to be flexible and to understand how other departments work are essential in leadership.

> **8** Make friends with people in different departments, and get to know how they operate.

BROADENING KNOWLEDGE

Use your experience in multidisciplinary project teams to broaden your general business skills. It is too easy to become and stay a specialist. The Japanese, for instance, believe that every manager should be a complete businessman or woman, able to lead any part of the business successfully. So a personnel head can move easily into sales, or a finance expert into marketing. Get to understand the principles of business and what part each component skill plays in achieving sales and profits. Broaden your knowledge by reading, and by establishing and nurturing contacts in different departments – such efforts will pay great dividends later.

LEARNING NEW SKILLS ON A PROJECT

How to approach the project

How to communicate its objectives

Where to acquire resources

How to put resources to best use

How to liaise with other departments

How to negotiate

How to monitor performance

How to troubleshoot

How to achieve project goals

MASTERING ROLES

Leadership is a multidimensional function, requiring knowledge and understanding of many organizational needs. As a leader, you must master the various roles that are required to handle different people and circumstances with skill and efficiency.

9 Think carefully about the best way to behave in every situation.

10 Concentrate on getting things done, not on trying to show that you are the one in charge.

TAKING THE OVERVIEW

A leader's role differs materially from that of a manager. While a manager must focus on implementing specific tasks, the leader must act as a grandmaster, a strategist, directing the game as a whole, and organizing the players. All leaders have different talents, and may be stronger in some skills than in others. To be successful you must be able to fill a number of roles, using a range of skills and leadership styles according to the task, the situation, and the people involved.

BEING AN ADMINISTRATOR

Administration is a key role of the leader, and nowadays there is much more to the role than simply "sailing a tight ship" on a predetermined course. The modern administrator is expected to be creative, devising processes and streamlining activities, not only to ensure the smooth-running of procedures, but also to increase efficiency. To get the best from your team, set aside time to organize systems that will minimize time-wasting and improve productivity. Look for ways to reduce paperwork – direct communication is usually more effective. Liaise with other departments to ensure that everyone knows what is expected of them, and keep an open team diary for instant checks on current tasks and deadlines.

QUESTIONS TO ASK YOURSELF

Q Do I communicate directly with my team and also with other departments?

Q Am I sure that every member of the team understands his or her role fully?

Q Am I setting sufficiently ambitious goals?

Q Do I have procedures in place that allow me to check on team progress instantly?

Q Am I constantly looking for new ways to improve efficiency and productivity?

COMPARING LEADERS AND MANAGERS

LEADERS	MANAGERS
Administer	Implement
Originate	Copy
Develop	Maintain
Inspire trust	Control
Think long term	Think short term
Ask what and why	Ask how and when
Watch the horizon	Watch bottom line
Challenge status quo	Accept status quo
Are their own people	Are good soldiers
Do the right thing	Do things right

BECOMING A STRATEGIST

As a leader you need to focus on the wider issues that may affect your team's effectiveness, as well as the day-to-day business of getting things done. With your team, plan what you want to achieve in a given time, and break this down into attainable goals and objectives, ensuring that everyone is aware of their responsibilities. Unexpected problems may require adjustments to elements of the plan, so always leave plenty of room for revision.

11 Keep a checklist of key leadership duties and ensure that you do them.

Promoter of change

Administrator

Communicator

Expert

Strategist

12 Always look beyond the detail and consider the bigger picture.

◀ **FULFILLING KEY ROLES**
A leader must be a good communicator who cares for staff; an expert who is knowledgeable in his or her field; a strategist who looks to the future; an administrator who gets things done; and a proponent of change.

PROMOTING CHANGE

Change is vital for success in the future. By seeking to lead change, you are helping your organization to remain competitive and grow, and creating opportunities for individuals to enrich their careers and personal lives. Dare to be different – if everyone in your industry is stuck in the same pattern, search for changes that will be welcomed by customers and that will enable you to stand out. Encourage staff to generate ideas for change, and involve your team in the planning and implementation of change programs.

13 If you are resisting change, ask yourself why.

▼ **INSTIGATING CHANGE**
To ensure minimum disruption, communicate every aspect of a change to those concerned as soon as possible. Stress the positive aspects of the change, and gain commitment from others through your own dedication to the project.

| Communicate | Reassure | Stand firm |

FOCUSING ON PEOPLE

The effective management of others is paramount to success. As a leader you must be, and be seen to be, a people person who has the best interests of staff, as well as the organization, at heart. Seek to develop a climate of openness in which people are not afraid to express their opinions and share their ideas with you. Constantly encourage them to adopt the values and behavior that help the team and the organization to reach its goals. Above all, ensure that your people get the training they need to achieve their maximum potential.

Leader suggests a training course to help team members improve skills

◀ **BEING AN EXPERT**
As leader, you should possess an in-depth knowledge of your chosen field. Ensure that your staff have all the technical skills needed to enable them to perform effectively.

EVALUATING KEY LEADERSHIP ROLES

KEY ROLES	HOW TO FULFILL THEM

EXPERT
Has in-depth understanding of his/her field.

- Strive for the best possible performance, and increase your knowledge in your specific field.
- Use your expertise to improve technical performance and technological strength in key areas.

ADMINISTRATOR
Ensures the smooth running of operations.

- Cut down on paperwork, and devise progressive systems to increase efficiency.
- Set rules, systems, boundaries, and values in order to ensure effective control.

PEOPLE PERSON
Makes staff and their training a top priority.

- Believe and act on the principle that success flows from the effective management of others.
- Seek to develop a climate of openness, and work with, and for, everybody equally.

STRATEGIST
Thinks long term and looks to the future.

- Always ensure that you plan ahead, devising strategies and goals for future success.
- Concentrate systematically on where the organization needs to go and how it will get there.

CHANGE AGENT
Uses change as a key to progress and advancement.

- Be adventurous, and endeavor to focus on enterprise and initiative rather than control.
- Seek to lead change, and actively encourage the generation of new ideas in others.

USING DIFFERENT STYLES

There are many different leadership styles, and to be truly effective in any given situation, you should not only be aware of them all, but be able to use elements of each simultaneously. For example, while managing and developing people, you still need to keep your eye on the strategic future at all times. If you are implementing a major change program, do not neglect your administrative duties or you run the risk of being unable to implement the changes effectively.

14 The greater your expertise, the more authority you will have.

DEVELOPING STRENGTHS

All the attributes that you will require as a leader can be developed – even drive and energy. Self-confidence and self-determination, combined with an ability to manage people and money, will make you a strong leader able to attain your targets.

15 Always work on and build upon your own strengths.

SETTING HIGH GOALS

You cannot hope to achieve without the self-confidence to take risks, which should be carefully calculated, on paper, to ensure that they are acceptable. This will enhance your ability to form high but realistic and achievable goals. Evaluation on paper helps put you in control of your own destiny, and will aid long-term vision of your own future and that of the business.

16 Put all your ambitions down on paper to help you realize them.

ELIMINATING WEAKNESSES

Facing up to your own mistakes and weaknesses is the first step toward eliminating them and raising your leadership ability. You may need help from a mentor, as well as feedback from your people. List aspects of your people management that are unsatisfactory, and determine how to improve them. Ultimate success means getting others to work with you and for you productively.

17 Understand what you are doing in order to achieve your aims.

MASTERING FIGURES

Some leaders are uncomfortable with money. If this applies to you, make sure you take a course. No sensible employer will refuse to pay for this education. There is no substitute, though, for sitting down and working out the figures of a real business, and seeing in real life how reality is reflected and portrayed by the numbers.

18 Never accept any weakness as one that you cannot correct and cure.

BUILDING PERSONAL STRENGTHS

STRENGTHS	HOW TO DEVELOP THEM
DRIVE AND ENERGY The ability to put maximum mental and physical effort behind reaching objectives and to keep going until the aims are achieved.	● Keep physically fit. Join a gym or take up a competitive sport. ● Constantly work through lists of tasks and ensure their completion.
SELF-CONFIDENCE A belief in your ability to carry out self-appointed and other tasks to your satisfaction and that of colleagues.	● Learn to calculate and accept moderate risks. ● Review your work at frequent intervals, comparing plans with outcomes.
MONEY MANAGEMENT Knowing how to read balance sheets, draw up budgets and management accounts, and track paths to higher profits.	● Acquire good training in financial basics – attend a course if necessary. ● Always work out financial consequences of plans and decisions in detail.
MANAGING PEOPLE Understanding how to get the best from your staff, and encouraging them to use their initiative to achieve better results.	● Ask regularly for feedback from your superiors, peers, and subordinates. ● Learn to look at situations through other people's eyes.
GOAL-SETTING Knowing how to set targets that are high enough to stimulate exceptional effort, but are still within achievement range.	● 'Benchmark' organizations in your own and other industries to see where and what improvements can be made. ● List your goals and keep reassessing them.
SELF-DETERMINATION The belief that your destiny and that of the business are in your hands, not subject to others or outside forces.	● Form long-range aims for yourself and the organization. ● Put your aims down on paper, complete with plans for implementation.
SELF-EVALUATION The ability to recognize and learn from mistakes and failures, while also analyzing the lessons of success.	● Conduct regular, honest examinations of recent decisions and actions. ● If you discover any weaknesses, draw up plans for rectifying them.
COMPETITIVENESS The will to win, and to take defeat as a challenge, not a disaster, coupled with the pursuit of high personal standards.	● Take every opportunity to study winners, corporate and individual. ● Adopt, adapt, and apply the techniques or qualities that make winners successful.

ASSESSING YOUR LEADERSHIP POTENTIAL

valuate how well you measure up as a prospective leader by responding to the following statements, and mark the options closest to your experience. If your answer is "never," mark Option 1; if it is "always," mark Option 4; and so on. Add your scores together, and refer to the Analysis to see how well you fared. Use your answers to identify the areas that most need improvement.

OPTIONS
1 Never
2 Occasionally
3 Frequently
4 Always

1 I take the lead in meetings to clarify objectives and agendas.

1 2 3 4

2 I focus strongly on achieving results from the tasks I undertake.

1 2 3 4

3 I propose original ideas for discussion in meetings.

1 2 3 4

4 I make friends easily and have many useful outside contacts.

1 2 3 4

5 I find and tell the objective truth, even if people don't like to hear it.

1 2 3 4

6 I maintain friendly relations with everyone on the team.

1 2 3 4

7 My ability makes me want to take charge.

1 2 3 4

8 I take advice impartially from above, below, and from equals.

1 2 3 4

9 I find it easy to express genuine, close friendship.

1 2 3 4

10 I like people to express genuine, close friendship with me.

1 2 3 4

11 I can work easily with all types of people.

1 2 3 4

12 I take time out each week to recharge my mental batteries.

1 2 3 4

ANALYSIS

Now that you have completed the self-assessment, add up your total score, and check your ability by reading the corresponding evaluation. However great your potential as a leader may be, remember that there is always room for improvement. Identify your weakest areas, and refer to the relevant sections in this book, where you will find practical advice and tips to help you understand what it takes to lead others and improve your leadership skills.

12–24: You are potentially competent, but you need to do a lot of work before you can excel in a leadership role.

25–36: Although you have the makings of a good leader, some areas still need to be improved. Identify and work on them.

37–48: Your leadership promise is high, but do not become complacent. Strive to realize it.

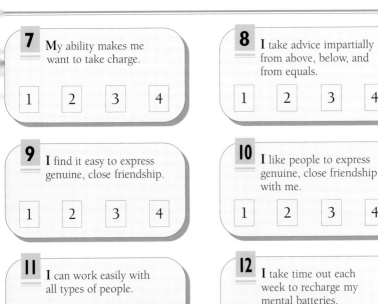

19

LEADING OTHERS

How well you lead others is the prime factor in your team's success. To be an effective leader, you must facilitate, inspire, and implement, rather than control.

PREPARING TO LEAD

L *eading others is a stimulating challenge*
for any leader. Get to know the people
who are working for you, establish a
framework in which everyone can operate
comfortably, and set challenging goals that
will motivate and inspire.

19 Take time to get your bearings in a new job – but do not take too long.

QUESTIONS TO ASK YOURSELF

Q What are we trying to achieve?

Q In what ways are we trying to achieve it?

Q What major issues do we face?

Q What do others think of the organization – good and bad?

Q Are we properly organized to achieve what we want in the way we want?

GATHERING INFORMATION

Your first priority as a leader, especially if you happen to be taking over a new situation, is to find out what you have, in terms of people, policies, problems, and opportunities. An excellent approach is to go around either all the people, or (in a larger organization) the key ones, and find out their views by asking questions. Discover what they think about the organization and what they are trying to achieve. Not only will you learn a great deal about your new responsibility, but the response to your questions will also teach you a great deal about the people concerned.

ESTABLISHING A FRAMEWORK

Every leader must think about the framework in which the leader and the led can operate effectively and comfortably, both as individuals and as part of a team. Ensure that there are systems in place that enable good, open communication between you and your staff. Be clear about the roles of each team member, and make sure that everyone is aware of their responsibilities.

> **20** Actively seek the views of your team members.

DO'S AND DON'TS

☑ Do use all means to communicate with your staff.

☑ Do strive to regard your associates as competent people.

☑ Do try to create a positive atmosphere, free from rigidity.

☑ Do show your staff loyalty and support.

☑ Do set challenging, ambitious goals.

☒ Don't ask people to do things that you wouldn't do yourself.

☒ Don't forget that trust is a two-way process that can take time and effort to establish.

☒ Don't take sides or show any favoritism.

☒ Don't dissuade staff from speaking out.

☒ Don't be vague about team members' roles.

ESTABLISHING OBJECTIVES

A leader must always be aware of the ultimate goals of the organization, and know how their own objectives fit in with them. Once these goals have been established, you must ensure that your team understands the direction in which they are heading and why, and the purpose of their own activities within the overall plan. The ultimate objective should be broken down into attainable, yet challenging goals that ideally will be inspiring and motivating for the whole team. Aims should also relate directly to the specific skills of each individual within the team. Working together toward a shared goal gives people a sense of ownership and responsibility, and builds an atmosphere of team spirit.

Leader meets with colleague personally to obtain feedback

◀ **TALKING TO STAFF**
The leader should talk to colleagues personally in order to discover their views. This results in useful feedback that will help the team to work more effectively.

FORMING THE BEST TEAM

Establishing a team or appointing new team members is the responsibility of the leader. Find the best candidates to form a balanced and dynamic team, either through internal promotion or external recruitment, and help them to feel part of the team.

21 Avoid appointing a candidate simply because you are short-staffed.

22 When recruiting team members, look for their growth potential.

▼ **RECRUITING STAFF**
There are many channels for recruiting people, and all of them should be explored. However, personal contacts are most likely to succeed.

FINDING CANDIDATES

Cast the widest possible net, and spend as much time as needed on the selection process. Draw up a list of criteria, essential characteristics, and skills that the appointee must have. Make sure that the criteria are relevant. A common mistake is to insist on "industry experience", when research shows that it bears little relationship to success in the job. Candidates who fulfill all your criteria will be rare, so be prepared to be flexible at the selection stage.

Advertise in relevant press for applicants

Recruit from within your organization

Approach local colleges for new recruits

Ask friends and colleagues for suggestions

Recruit from government training schemes

Commission an agency to find best candidates

PROMOTING INSIDERS

Internal promotion is not only cheaper, but tells everybody that they have the opportunity to rise, which is the most satisfying form of reward. Leaders should constantly be on the lookout for abilities that can be exploited in higher-level teams. When recruiting internally, give consideration to the morale of other staff, who may feel that they have been passed over. Explain clearly to all concerned why the person that you selected is right for this assignment, and emphasize that there will be other opportunities. Then allow your candidate to prove you right.

BALANCING SKILLS

For any team to function effectively, there must be a balance of technical, problem-solving, decision-making, and interpersonal skills among its members. The ideal group will be creative yet disciplined, able to generate new ideas and find solutions to difficulties, and, at the same time, organized enough to plan and implement a task within a given period.

23 Take into account the feelings of staff when promoting internally.

Leader announces that staff member has been promoted

Newly promoted member of team seeks colleague's support

Employee congratulates colleague on appointment

◀ MAKING AN INTERNAL APPOINTMENT
Announce the appointment to staff and ensure that they understand your reasons for selecting the candidate.

24 When a referee has reservations, always probe more deeply.

25 Ask candidates what they did really well in their previous jobs.

26 Ensure there are no interruptions during interviews.

CONDUCTING INTERVIEWS

Allow 45 minutes for an interview, preferably with one colleague, or at most, two, joining in. Keep your own talking to a minimum. You want the candidate to say as much as possible about their understanding of the job, your company, their past performance. What did they do best? You are interested in their strengths first, weaknesses second. Observe them carefully, taking into account body language and appearance.

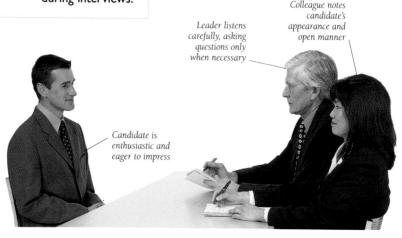

Leader listens carefully, asking questions only when necessary

Colleague notes candidate's appearance and open manner

Candidate is enthusiastic and eager to impress

JUDGING SUITABILITY

Psychometric tests and handwriting analysis (graphology) are sometimes used to evaluate candidates' suitability. But these methods are no substitute for personal judgment, reinforced by the person's track record and references, and by any appropriate skill tests. Conflicts and rivalry within groups are counterproductive, so avoid candidates who display a degree of personal assertiveness that may fracture the team spirit.

▲ ASSESSING A CANDIDATE

Observe the candidate carefully. Keep your checklist of attributes and skills in front of you, and make sure that you address them all. Above all, do not ignore your intuition or your personal reaction – it is very important that you actually like the candidate. Ask yourself whether the candidate seems "nice" and if he or she will fit in.

LEARNING FROM RECRUITS

A leader can learn a great deal from new recruits by exploiting their knowledge of other organizations, methods, or ideas. They have the advantage of an outsider's eye, before being assimilated into your company's ways. Make time for conversations with recruits, asking them for their first impressions. Acting on their suggestions is an important way of promoting their confidence.

27 See that new recruits are welcomed and fully supported.

Leader asks recruit for her impressions of the company

Colleague sits in on meeting

◆ EASING IN RECRUITS
Help new employees to learn about their new environment and master the work by appointing a suitable colleague to act as "nursemaid" while they settle in.

QUESTIONS TO ASK YOURSELF

Q What did I do wrong – did I recruit poorly?

Q Did the person lack the necessary support?

Q Have circumstances changed so that the person no longer fits the original job?

Q Is there another job in which they could succeed?

HANDLING MISFITS

Recruitment failures will inevitably occur, however much care has been taken. Whenever you contemplate dismissing somebody, always ask yourself "why has this happened?". Learn from your analysis, and if the person can be "saved" by making changes, make them. If not, do not allow the person to stay after you have, consciously or subconsciously, decided against it. Explain your reasons fully to the individual, and be as generous as possible in negotiating severance. Also, ensure that coworkers know what has happened and why.

EXERCISING AUTHORITY

The role of a leader is to ensure that everyone understands instructions and carries them out effectively. Since it is rare for everything to go according to plan, put into place reporting systems that enable you to deal with any deviations swiftly.

28 Make sure that any instructions you give are clear and concise.

29 Encourage people to approach you if things go wrong.

30 Act quickly when you learn of any real problems.

GIVING INSTRUCTIONS

The method of giving instructions matters far less than the quality of their content. If a decision has been reached in concert with the team, the leader has no need to win acceptance. But having to say "This is an order" is a sign of malfunction on one side or the other. Before you issue instructions, be absolutely clear in your own mind what your requirements are. This will be reflected in your tone of voice and body language and will reinforce your message. Ask people if they have any reservations about what you have asked of them, so that problems can be cleared up at the outset.

MANAGING BY EXCEPTION

Leaders often spend too much time double-checking everything to ensure conformance with instructions and procedures. The better approach is to manage by exception, which involves concentrating on what is going awry rather than what is not. You should not expect to hear about actions that proceed as planned, but staff or delegates should inform you immediately if there is a serious deviation from the plan. For example, if a sales executive is asked to handle key accounts, and sales targets or profit margins are being missed, he or she must report the problem to you at once.

Marketing director reports that the month's sales of an important product have fallen substantially

BEING CONSISTENT

Since leadership is about getting other people to do what you want, it is essential to maintain the cooperation and respect of your staff. Be consistent in the way you exercise authority, so that people can trust you and know that you mean what you say. This avoids ambiguity, and the danger of ill-feeling or resentment developing is reduced. Being consistent does not mean being overindulgent toward staff – as long as you are always honest, direct, and fair in your dealings with other people, they will respond positively to your authority, even under difficult or stressful circumstances.

31 Insist that staff tell you all the news, good or bad.

32 Use crises as an opportunity to develop people.

Leader asks production boss to report capacity bottlenecks in future

A plan is devised to divert unused capacity for another product, and to raise output to meet the unsatisfied demand

Leader is told that shortfall is caused by lack of capacity

Leader discovers that production is down. He calls in production boss

▲ ORGANIZING CONTROLS

By putting into place a new reporting system, the leader ensures that, in future, he will be aware of any production problems before they affect sales.

DELEGATING TASKS

*As leader, you should concentrate your
time on activities that nobody else can
do. Delegation is a form of time management.
It is a way of exercising control and meeting
your own responsibilities more effectively,
while developing the skills of your staff.*

33 Remember that delegation boosts morale and builds confidence.

34 Never keep work simply because you do it better.

35 Set high targets in agreement with your delegates.

INCREASING YOUR TIME

Managers often claim that the demands of operational and routine duties leave them little time to concentrate on important, long-term matters, such as strategic planning and training. To create more time for yourself, it is essential to hand down more routine tasks by delegation. Even if you, the leader, are better and faster at a task than anybody else in the team, the golden rule is that you should not, and cannot, do everything yourself. Leadership involves handing over the task to others, and then helping them to match or exceed your standards.

BRIEFING DELEGATES

Give the delegate a clear, written brief, developed in consultation, that sets out the objectives, the resources available, the constraints, and the time schedule, if relevant. Supplement the written brief with an interview to ensure mutual understanding. If the circumstances change, alter the brief to suit – do not stick to it slavishly.

Delegate seeks clarification on unclear points

Leader asks delegate to summarize key points of brief

EXPLAINING THE BRIEF ▶
Make sure that the delegate fully understands the assignment by asking relevant questions at a face-to-face meeting. Invite the delegate to do the same.

SUPERVISING EFFECTIVELY

Allow the delegate to develop and execute his or her plans, subject only to keeping you fully informed. Constant interference, countermanding decisions and actions taken by the delegate, and checking up continually all add up to poor leadership. By intervening heavily, you will also frustrate the delegate and deny him or her the chance to learn new skills and gain experience. Monitor the progress of the work with a system of written reports and face-to-face meetings with the delegate, and by observing performance.

36 If time pressure increases, ask if you are delegating enough to others.

37 Check regularly and informally on progress of delegated tasks.

REINFORCING A DELEGATE'S ROLE ▼

Always introduce a new delegate to existing team members, as this will help him or her to feel part of the team. It is also important to inform any customers or suppliers who need to know what specific responsibilities the new delegate will have.

New delegate is made to feel welcome

Leader introduces new delegate and clearly states her responsibilities

Team member understands new delegate's role within team

RETAINING TASKS

There are some responsibilities that a leader cannot delegate. These include key areas, such as controlling overall performance, meeting strategic objectives, and confidential human resources matters – how people are rewarded, appraised, promoted, informed, disciplined, coached, and counseled. You may also need to supervise dealings with important customers if delegating ultimate responsibility for these contacts would endanger the relationship.

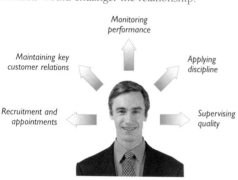

Monitoring performance

Maintaining key customer relations

Applying discipline

Recruitment and appointments

Supervising quality

◀ **KEEPING KEY TASKS**
As a leader, you must keep charge of sensitive matters, such as applying discipline and making appointments, and retain control of important areas, including finance and strategy.

---

38 Keep an open door for all your delegates.

39 Intervene fast when the delegate cannot cope.

PROVIDING SUPPORT

An open-door policy aids effective delegation. The delegate should be able to approach the delegator at any time for advice, information, or revision. The delegator should also be able to approach the delegate, whenever necessary, for an informal, encouraging discussion on how the task is going. If the delegator visits too often, either this is bad delegation, or the delegation is going badly. If delegates come through the door too often, they are either insecure or inadequate. If you are confident in their ability, give them a clear message: "I am confident that you can manage."

CHECKING PROGRESS WITH DELEGATES

When discussing progress with delegates, use positive questions, such as those below, that will encourage delegates to suggest their own solutions to problems. Avoid questions that may discourage or demoralize the delegate.

❝ Is there anything you want to bring to my notice? ❞

❝ We failed to meet that target. Any suggestions as to how that might have happened? ❞

❝ I see that costs are over-running. What steps are you taking to bring them back in line? ❞

❝ How do you think we can avoid making this mistake again? ❞

DEVELOPING DELEGATES

40 Make sure that everybody knows what must always be left to you.

Look out for signs that the delegate is taking too much on his or her own shoulders, and not allowing people who work for them to show initiative and tackle their own tasks without interference. "Getting out of the way" is the key to getting the best from others, and applies to the delegate too. Encourage delegates to think issues through and come up with answers to problems before bringing them to you. The most important lesson for the delegate is that of being accountable for results, with no opportunity for excuses.

CASE HISTORY
John was working for a new boss in a new company and a new country. He was given the task of organizing a new project team, complete with an excellent brief. But problems arose. With existing resources, there was no hope of meeting the production targets from internal supply, as ordered. He went back to his American boss, Chuck, with the problem – and was disconcerted by the response.

"I don't want people bringing me problems without solutions," said Chuck. "I want two solutions every time, with your recommendation on which one to take. If you ever bust in here without the two solutions, you'll leave the office a damn sight faster than you came in." John went away and returned with two solutions: subcontract some of the work, or ask for more finance and people. He preferred the first, and so did Chuck.

◀ ENCOURAGING SOLUTIONS
Being a good delegator, the leader in this case did not want his people to become dependent on him and his decisions. So he forced them to make up their own minds. The boss was still prepared to discuss the issue, but his insistence helped this subordinate to be a real leader.

COMMUNICATING CLEARLY

The ability to communicate with staff is essential in leadership. To ensure that messages are received and understood all the way down, flatten the hierarchy of your team structure. To keep communication two-way, invite feedback from your staff.

41 Talk honestly with your staff and you will get honest answers in return.

COMMUNICATING DIRECTLY

The leader at the apex of the hierarchy passes down information and instructions, level by level, throughout the team. The trouble with this top-down management style is that you cannot always be sure that your message has gone through, or how it has been received, since there is little feedback from the lower levels. Wherever possible, deliver your message in person to ensure that it has been clearly understood by the recipient.

42 Take steps to get accurate reports of team opinions.

▼ **FLATTENING THE HIERARCHY**
You need only three levels of hierarchy and four types of staff. Leaders work in concert with managers, while staff take charge of their own output. All three levels are assisted by experts, such as information technology specialists.

ENTERPRISE MANAGERS
Responsible for strategic direction and overall success of the organization

PEOPLE MANAGERS
Responsible for implementation and the rest of the employees

STAFF
Responsible for quality and quantity of own output

EXPERTS
Responsible for specific areas, such as finance, technologies, etc.

COMMUNICATING ON ALL LEVELS

To ensure that the right message has been received and the right action taken, the top-down process needs to be checked by bottom-up communication. Spend as much time as possible with all levels of staff, and make it clear that you appreciate feedback and are willing to listen and respond. Remember that excellent ideas can come from anywhere, and are not just confined to leaders. Make use of the fact that other people know their own area of work, and can make an invaluable contribution to related issues.

COMMUNICATION

- Customers
- Staff
- Managers

▲ INVERTING THE PYRAMID

Some leaders mentally balance the pyramid on its point to reverse the direction of the flow of information. Customers and their needs are put on top, followed by the employees, then the managers.

---

43 If all feedback is positive, you may not have been told the whole truth.

44 Be prepared for misunderstanding of what you are trying to achieve.

LISTENING TO STAFF

Encourage people to be open and honest with you by showing that you value their opinions and are willing to listen to them. The best way to do this is through informal conversations, either one-on-one or with groups of staff. Make it clear that even negative feedback is viewed as a positive opportunity for improvement. You must ensure that staff are not intimidated by fear of any repercussions when they express criticisms. Do not always wait for staff to come to you – solicit feedback from them by asking for their comments on issues that affect them. If you want to gain a broad picture of staff attitudes, you will have to use a more formal approach. Many techniques are available, such as surveys, sample polling, suggestion boxes, or focus groups.

DYNAMIZING GROUPS

To dynamize a group, you must give it strong purpose, strong membership, and strong leadership. Use "hot groups" for special operations, choosing the ablest and most motivated candidates for the group. Encourage innovation and creativity.

45 Encourage groups to achieve by setting high but realistic targets.

IMPARTING PURPOSE

A group of people striving toward a common goal should be highly motivated, with a strong sense of excitement and anticipation. The way that you, as leader, convey the purpose of the task to your group can help to instill this positive attitude. Emphasize the fact that the group has been put together for a specific purpose, and that the particular skills of each individual member are fundamental to the success of the project. This helps people to identify with the organization's goals, and empowers them to use their creativity.

ROUSING THE TROOPS

Talking to a group as a unit provides an essential test of leadership quality. Be positive and enthusiastic – your energy will inspire confidence and encourage your group to follow your example. While it is important to put across your personality, policies, and objectives, you should also reinforce group identity by providing plenty of opportunities for discussion and debate. Be firm about your expectations, but remember that enjoyment is a key motivator.

Colleague takes opportunity to state his opinion

Team member enjoys being part of dynamic group

STAYING FOCUSED ▶
Hold regular meetings to inform everyone of what has been achieved and how much more needs to be done. Use these times to reinforce motivation and purpose.

FORMING HOT GROUPS

Nothing is more exciting in management than leading a "hot group," a team assembled for a special operation, such as a new product launch. Success requires finding the ablest people and placing them under highly motivated, effective leadership (which encourages sub-leadership). The group continues to recruit talent as a key activity, concentrating on people who are right for each job and can share a powerful vision. It helps to detach the group from all other operations, and to focus change on a chosen rival: "the enemy."

Team member is encouraged by leader's positive approach

Leader encourages constructive debate

BRIEFING HOT GROUPS

Introduce the subject
(and yourself, if
appropriate)

↓

Announce the
objective

↓

Express confidence
in the people present

↓

Emphasize
group/team working

↓

Look forward,
not backward

↓

Put across your
authority

↓

Express confidence in
the group's ability

↓

Banish doubt
and doubters

↓

Emphasize that efforts
will be fully supported

COLLEGIATE LEADERSHIP

Are you a "man on horseback" or a first among equals? The first kind of leader is the military model; the second is the collegiate model. The collegiate style is increasingly winning, since it promotes a sense of unity and motivation within a company.

46 Always be ready to allow others to take the lead when appropriate.

47 Remember that everyone in a team thinks in a different way.

LEADING AS AN EQUAL

The first-among-equals model is formalized in German business, where the chief executive is called the "spokesman" of the management board. The reason why this approach is spreading is because many minds are more powerful than one. Create a pool of shared talent and an environment of total communication, and consult all team members before an important decision is made. Even in small organizations, the range of expertise required has expanded greatly, probably beyond the reach of one individual. At particular stages, moreover, one of your experts should have the decisive voice by virtue of his or her expertise.

MEETING AS EQUALS ▼
Working with genuine colleagues demands the same behavior whether or not you are the leader. Respect goes to expertise, not to rank or seniority. Do not engage in internal politics, but focus on what will achieve the group's objectives, in the knowledge that everybody benefits from a job well done.

Expert gives technical assessment of issue

Colleague evaluates specialist information

Leader invites expert to give her opinion

Team member checks anger and lowers his voice

Leader calms down both parties

Colleague begins to feel less distressed

HANDLING ▶ DISPUTES
When colleagues seriously disagree, you should intervene to discover what is at issue. No matter what the provocation, never lose your temper. Anger is a bad adviser.

RESOLVING DIFFICULTIES

Even successful partnerships can develop disagreements. When resolving an issue, whether involving yourself or between colleagues, try to analyze the situation calmly. Start with the team's objective. Is it shared by the combatants? If so, what factual points are at issue? If they can be resolved, what are the emotional problems that are preventing agreement? You may conclude that one of the parties, or perhaps both, is intransigent and has lost sight of the aims. If you cannot persuade them to alter their attitude, they will have to leave the team.

48 Seek to defuse emotion before tackling issues.

49 Treating everyone equally will avoid causing resentment.

SEEKING THE ▶ BEST OUTCOME
The leader in this case faced a real conflict between valued members of staff. It was important not to take sides, and to see that the best solution for the company was found. Involving another member of the team got to the real issue, and the leader was able to bring this out into the open and make a clear decision.

CASE STUDY

Roger, in charge of distribution, and Ann, customer services manager, put forward two rival plans for reorganizing the marketing department. Neither would accept the other's arguments. Their boss, Barry, asked Norman, manager of new product development and an excellent analyst, to examine the two plans. The report came down strongly in favor of Ann's ideas. Confronted with the choice, Roger still refused to agree: the reorganization would mean that he reported to Ann, and he did not want to work for a woman. Barry confronted him with this blockage and gave him a choice: accept or leave. Roger argued that his plan had been unfairly treated. Barry brought Norman into the meeting and asked him to give his reasons. Reluctantly, Roger accepted the logic and stayed.

IMPROVING YOUR EFFECTIVENESS

The best leaders seek constantly to improve and develop their skills. For the greatest success and impact, it is essential to work on upgrading and extending the basic techniques.

MAKING DECISIONS

All decisions involve a series of other decisions, notably when to settle the issue, who else to involve in the decision-making process, and what alternatives to consider. Get these decisions right and you will be poised to make the correct move.

> **50** If you can safely make a decision quickly, always do so.

TIMING DECISIONS

What kind of decision do you face? Time is the starting point. Does your decision have to be made immediately, by a later deadline, or at your discretion? Making no decision is a decision in itself, and possibly a fateful one. If you take no action, the time may come when an urgent decision is demanded, but it may be too late to undo the damage caused by inaction. Usually, the sooner a decision is made, the better. Even if you do not know what to do, always avoid procrastination. Seek guidance from a trusted colleague or superior, then decide on the best course of action.

Colleague expresses his opinions

CONSIDERING ALL OPTIONS

Some decisions make themselves. Other decisions have either/or choices. Others have multiple options. For decisions with two or more alternatives, be systematic in your approach. Take time to list all the available options and assess their validity and likely consequences – if necessary, involve others to generate ideas and gather relevant information. Only when you have fully researched all the options are you in a good position to select a course of action.

51 If you ask for advice from a coworker, expect to act on it.

SEEKING CONSENSUS

Involving others in the decision-making process requires method. The normal Western system is to debate the issue and to argue about the pros and cons of the alternatives. The Eastern way is for each participant to state his or her opinion in turn, without debate. Either way, encourage people to speak their minds. Then summarize the options and seek whatever degree of consensus is possible. Above all, finally decide yourself.

▼ **SHARING DECISIONS**

Discussing a problem with colleagues and analyzing the alternatives together is often the best way to move toward a decision.

Leader listens to colleague's views before making final decision himself

SEEING DECISIONS THROUGH

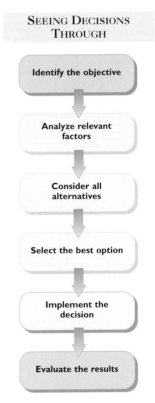

Identify the objective

↓

Analyze relevant factors

↓

Consider all alternatives

↓

Select the best option

↓

Implement the decision

↓

Evaluate the results

SETTING AMBITIOUS GOALS

Goals are the essence of planning, whether for the long, medium, or short terms. They should be ambitious but achievable. Set stretching, hard-headed, but feasible sub-goals to help your team attain their ultimate goal.

52 Seek to turn the impossible into a target that you can achieve.

TESTING CRITERIA FOR GOALS

- Are they clear, hard, and measurable?
- Are they approved by the implementers?
- Can they realistically be achieved?
- Do they have a clear, sensible timeframe?
- Have they been translated into full plans?
- Will they be revised as events dictate?
- Will reaching them advance our strategy?
- Will they generate rewards for people?
- Do they translate into individual goals?

BEING AMBITIOUS

The degree of ambition in setting goals is important because people respond to the promise of high achievement, in sports and business alike. A leader who thinks big can prove that what seemed unrealistic and impossible to achieve is actually within everyone's grasp. Set goals whose accomplishment will fill team members with pride and observers with admiration.

AIMING FOR THE MOON ▶
Every leader needs to seek the equivalent of President Kennedy's commitment of America to 'go to the moon'. If you think small, you will probably not achieve big results, even by accident.

SELECTING OBJECTIVES

OBJECTIVES **TARGETS** **ULTIMATE GOAL**

Reduce the price → Lower the costs of manufacture and distribution

Offer customers better value → Improve the product

Change methods to meet the objectives → Set targets and timescales for teams and individuals

→ Increase in market share

▲ ACHIEVING ENDGOALS

By selecting your objectives, individuals and teams can be given targets and timescales that, if achieved, will come together to meet the ultimate goal.

SETTING OBJECTIVES

Goals are seldom met without having to overcome unexpected difficulties, disappointments, and even disasters. Achieving your aims despite such setbacks is a crucial test of leadership. First, do not panic or blame. Neither will help to get the plan back on track, if that still remains feasible. You should take immediate action to deal swiftly and surely with the negative event and its consequences. Remember that a positive state of mind is crucial in reaching goals, so try to instill this in your team.

REVISING GOALS

If you suffer a setback, reassess the viability of the goal as soon as possible. Does it need serious revision? Must more time and/or money be allowed? You may have to abandon the goal – but take this step only if dispassionate analysis shows it to be the only practical alternative. Try to use the setback as a trigger to stimulate renewed effort by being positive and decisive yourself.

53 Expect setbacks, and always have contingency plans fully prepared.

54 Cut your losses fast if failure is truly inevitable.

DEVELOPING TEAMWORK

For a team to work well, several roles must be played – not independently, but collectively. The leader's role is to develop a team that thinks and acts together, with individual and team interests aligned.

55 Ensure that team members share the same goals.

ASSIGNING ROLES

The efficient team consists of people who can play several key roles (including coordinator, critic, ideas person, implementer, external contact, inspector, and team builder) in addition to the skills they bring to the basic tasks of the team. As leader, ensure that all these roles are played, sometimes with people combining roles. When organizing the team, fit the roles to the talents available, and provide training if necessary.

DEVELOPING TEAM LEADERSHIP SKILLS

To be an effective team leader, you must:
- Ensure that everyone on the team is working toward agreed, shared objectives;
- Criticize constructively, and make sure that you praise good work as well as find fault;
- Monitor the team members' activities continuously by obtaining effective feedback;
- Constantly encourage and organize the generation of new ideas within the team;
- Always insist on the highest standards of execution from team members;
- Develop the individual and collective skills of the team, and seek to strengthen them by training and recruitment.

KEY TEAM ROLES

COORDINATOR
Pulls together the work of the team as a whole.

CRITIC
Guardian and analyst of the team's effectiveness.

IDEAS PERSON
Encourages the team's innovative vitality.

IMPLEMENTER
Ensures smooth-running of the team's actions.

EXTERNAL CONTACT
Looks after the team's external contacts.

INSPECTOR
Ensures that high standards are maintained.

TEAM BUILDER
Develops the team spirit.

MULTITASKING

Teams can function well in a situation where each member has a specific task and does nothing else. But in many cases you need more flexibility, which is when multitasking becomes important. Teams function better when people understand each other's jobs. Allocate time for your team members to work with others on the team. For example, encourage a production worker to accompany a salesperson to see a customer, or sit a marketing person next to an engineer. This broadens perceptions as well as skills, and promotes cooperation.

56 Encourage competition between ideas, not individuals.

POINTS TO REMEMBER

- Roles should be matched to personality rather than the personality pushed into the role.
- If a team has only a few members, roles can be doubled or tripled up to ensure that the team's needs are covered.
- Once roles have been allocated, consult the team members to get their agreement on what needs to be done and how.
- Specific tasks should be allocated to each team member, complete with time scales and reporting responsibilities.
- Performance must be monitored at team meetings.
- It is important to concentrate on collective achievement.
- Individual contributions should be dealt with in a team context.

▲ BUILDING A STRONGER TEAM
Provide the training that enables people to master more than one task, and then your multiskilled team members can be used as understudies and as coworkers when help is needed.

57 Boost a team's effectiveness by training members in new skills.

EMPOWERING TEAMS

Empower team members by giving them whole tasks and allowing them to find the best way of performing them, but make any suggestions you feel necessary for improvement. In this way you are enabling them to use their talents more fully. Let everybody exercise the right to think and contribute their intelligence to the team.

▲ **TAKING A BACK SEAT**
As leader, step back and let team members take the lead when appropriate. You do not have to chair every meeting or make every decision. The more you encourage the team to develop and use leadership skills, the stronger your own leadership will be.

58 Ask people if they have enough responsibility.

59 Do not accept the opinions of others on team abilities.

INHERITED TEAMS

If you inherit a team, or have its membership decided for you, do not jump to conclusions about the members until you have got to know them reasonably well and have understood their present capabilities. Set aside time to talk to each team member, one-on-one, about their individual tasks, their ideas, and their views of their own performance. This will give you a clear insight into their characters and abilities. You can then decide what roles and tasks are appropriate, and whether any training is needed.

UNDERSTANDING REWARDS

Rewards for good performance can take several forms, including pay raises, bonuses, profit-sharing programs, stock options, and recognition such as vacations or prizes. The object of a reward program is to motivate teams and individuals to perform even better. Good leadership also recognizes that team members deserve to share financially in the success that they have created. The best idea is to let employees help to decide how bonus payments should be made.

60 Allow new people and teams to prove how good they are.

REWARDING INDIVIDUALS

There is a conflict between the interests of the team and those of the individual. For example, if an individual asks for a pay raise and you meet their demand, you must expect the team to learn what has happened. If they feel the raise is unfair, that might disrupt teamworking. You cannot be unfair to an individual because of the perceptions of other team members. Be frank, explain your decision fully, and stand by it.

61 Reward real merit openly, but never appear to play any favorites.

CHOOSING A REWARD SYSTEM

REWARD	IMPLEMENTATION	ADVANTAGES
SALARY INCREASES Increases in basic rate of pay, not directly related to performance.	Requires management to decide on overall salary scale and placing of particular jobs within the scale.	● Individuals know exactly where they stand financially. ● Can reduce element of competition within teams.
BONUSES One-time payments linked to performance or financial targets.	Can take several forms, such as sharing financial savings, but payments must be based on meaningful measures.	● Increases motivation and job satisfaction. ● Gives staff incentive for cost-cutting and quality drives.
PROFIT-SHARING An allocated share of the profits is split between employees.	Management must find a fair method of profit distribution, either on a corporate or divisional basis.	● Is an excellent motivator of individuals. ● Gives teams a sense of working towards common aim.
STOCK OWNERSHIP Gift of stocks or chance to buy them on preferential terms.	Any rewards are directly linked to corporate success, and are moving down from top levels in many corporations.	● Encourages long-term loyalty and a sense of involvement. ● Helps staff identify with overall group results.
RECOGNITION REWARDS Many options, including prizes, vacations, parties.	Care should be taken to avoid implying that performing to the highest standards is the exception rather than the rule.	● Can reward teams or individuals. ● Staff are highly motivated by recognition, even if only verbal.
COMPOSITE REWARDS Rewards allocated for individual, team, and company results.	Allows management to combine individual with company-wide rewards, with elements tied to teamwork.	● Varying the reward packages keeps interest fresh. ● Recognition of teamwork elements boosts team spirit.

LEADING DISCUSSIONS

Whether they are formal or casual, involve groups of people, or are conducted on a one-on-one basis, discussions allow people to share ideas or concerns freely. By playing a leading role, you can keep discussions productive and purposeful.

TALKING TO YOUR TEAM

As a leader, you should call your team together on a regular basis to collect feedback, generate ideas, and make decisions. Even when holding small, informal discussions it is important to keep the purpose and a time limit in mind. Give people time to prepare, and make sure that everyone involved is given an opportunity to air their views. Encourage open conversation but discourage digressions and keep the subject matter moving forward toward an action agenda.

62 Give people a time for meetings and always keep the appointment.

QUESTIONS TO ASK YOURSELF

Q Am I seeking to give people information or instructions, or am I merely making an announcement?

Q Am I holding a discussion with the aim of making a decision or decisions?

Q Is the purpose to obtain feedback on progress?

Q Is it a negotiation or a disciplinary meeting?

Q Do I want to discuss long-term strategy?

Q Am I dealing with a short-term matter, perhaps a crisis?

Q Am I only trying to find the facts?

Member feels free to speak openly

▲ **MEETING INFORMALLY**
Informal one-to-one meetings provide opportunities to discuss issues frankly and reach decisions quickly. They also enable leaders to forge stronger relationships with individual members of staff.

63 Keep discussions informal whenever possible to ease staff relationships.

ENCOURAGING DISCUSSION

Facilitate personal contacts by organizing office space to give staff the chance to meet and exchange information. Extrawide corridors encourage casual discussions, as does sitting staff at round tables in open-plan offices. One company has elevators that stop at only one floor so that people must meet in them. Intranets and other networks achieve the same result electronically. This type of office contact is vital for sharing ideas and information, and for developing friendships.

▲ GETTING TOGETHER SOCIALLY

Events such as lunches, celebrations, and parties are important to foster easy exchanges of information and ideas. Socializing outside the office also helps to strike up friendships and smooth working relations between team members. As leader, you should be at the center of these circles, participating in them fully.

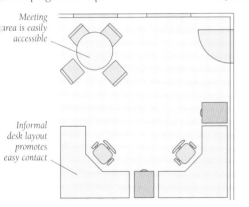

Meeting area is easily accessible

Informal desk layout promotes easy contact

▲ FOSTERING COMMUNICATION

An open-plan office is far more conducive to good communication than an enclosed, square-table office. In a more relaxed and informal setting, round tables are set aside for meetings in quieter areas away from desks. The important factor is to strike a balance between easy contact and efficiency.

CULTURAL DIFFERENCES

In order to facilitate discussion, some top bosses in the United States have abandoned executive suites for open-plan floors. The same can happen in Japan. Although individual offices hinder the flow of information, Germans and Britons still prefer them for reasons of prestige.

64 Never hide behind the closed doors of private offices.

USING MEETINGS

Organizations breed meetings, but often they lack any clear purpose. Ensure that meetings have valid goals – there is no point in bringing people together to rubber-stamp decisions that have already been made – and that they are time-effective.

65 Use meetings to take decisions as fast as possible, not to delay them.

66 Ask only relevant people to meetings to keep the numbers down.

67 Allow staff to stay away if they feel they have nothing to contribute.

MINIMIZING MEETINGS

Most leaders feel pressured by the amount of time that they are expected to spend in meetings. But how many meetings really serve a useful purpose? As leader, always consider the validity of a meeting before arranging it. Is it worth your own and others' time? For example, if you hold a weekly team meeting, does it serve a purpose or are you doing it purely out of habit?

QUESTIONING MEETINGS

To help you decide whether to call a meeting, assume that it is unnecessary unless it can pass the following triple test. Does the meeting have:
● A clearly defined purpose?
● Measurable outcomes?
● An entirely functional membership?
Used unwisely, meetings can reduce the opportunity for leadership because, instead of making decisions, meetings postpone them and dilute responsibility. Never use a meeting when individuals could do the same work.

RUNNING MEETINGS

Go into every meeting with a plan for what you want accomplished, while accepting that this may mean changing your own ideas. Except in emergencies, ensure that all documentation is distributed well before the meeting. In taking the chair, your role is to run an orderly discussion and to ensure that everybody who has something to say says it. End the meeting with a summary that includes an action plan, with deadlines and personal responsibilities for every action.

68 If you are in the chair, do not use the position to be dictatorial.

Leader keeps team standing to ensure meeting is brief

AVOIDING DELAYS

It is important that fixed meetings do not gum up the works. Learn from the example of a store chain that allows one manager to make decisions on a supplier's proposed price change on his own. A rival sends all these decisions to a pricing committee that meets every Monday. The result can be a seven-day delay, which could result in serious competitive loss. Leave similar authorizations to individuals wherever possible.

◀ **STANDING MEETINGS**
Follow the principle used by General Gus Pagonis, supply chief in the Gulf War. His morning meetings were literally standing. Since nobody was allowed to sit down, meetings were brief and to the point.

69 Keep meetings to the shortest time needed to cover a brief agenda.

ANALYZING PROBLEMS

The word problem means "something that is difficult to solve," "a puzzle," "something perplexing." By being positive and using analysis of the issue, you can overcome any obstacles and replace the problem with a solution.

70 Keep it simple and look first for the easy solution.

71 Regard problems as opportunities for team learning.

72 Consider an issue from every possible angle.

THINKING POSITIVELY

One leader found the word "problem" so negative that he banned its use. Instead of problems, managers were told to talk about opportunities. His attitude was right. The word problem really describes the need to choose between alternatives. If you are baffled, that is usually because you are unclear about what you want to accomplish, or because you are unwilling to accept the right alternative, even when analysis makes the best choice obvious. Recognizing the emotional blockage often helps the problem disappear.

EXAMINING THE FACTS

The issue could be isolated, such as whether to build a Web site. Or it may be recurrent, like how to control expenditure. In all cases, ask: What questions do I wish to answer? Why is there an issue? In pursuing the control issue, for example, you will want to know answers to the following questions: How much are the present controls costing? What benefits will result from change? What systems do others use? Who will supervise and who will devise the controls? What are the difficulties? What are the alternatives? Keep going until the questions run out. The answers will provide the essential facts, without which you cannot hope to generate the best solution.

73 Look for the positive side of any negative situation.

74 Ensure you have all the facts before taking action.

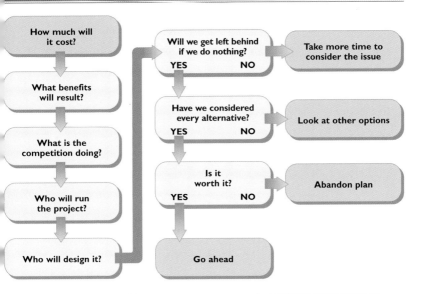

OVERCOMING OBSTACLES

Many issues tend to revolve around gaps. This means that there is a distance between where you are and where you want to be. The question is how to get from A to B. There may be a number of obstacles in your path, such as a shortage of resources (people or money, for example), powerful competitors, planning regulations, or many other snags. You can either explore ways of overcoming the obstacles or compromise on the objective. However, it is important that you do devise a plan for reaching your goal: only weak leaders, having identified the gap, take no action to close it.

▲ ASKING QUESTIONS
When attempting to resolve a problem, it is essential to ask yourself all the relevant questions. Once you have the answers available, the solution will follow.

▼ TAKING ACTION
Management writer Peter Drucker defines management as: "Knowing what to do; knowing how to do it, and doing it." The first two steps (Analysis and Planning) are useless without the third (Action).

GIVING SUPPORT

Trust can be difficult to build, but it is easy to lose. This is partly because people start with a distrustful mind-set. As a leader, you need to work hard at earning trust, fostering that trust by showing loyalty, and supporting your team fully.

75 Find ways of showing people that you trust them to act effectively.

POINTS TO REMEMBER

● If promises are made, they should always be kept.

● Going behind people's backs is not permissible.

● People should be kept fully informed of anything that might directly affect them.

● Performance should be judged and rewarded fairly.

BUILDING TRUST

Leaders have to prove themselves trustworthy by word and deed, and then prove themselves all over again. Even then, a few people will continue to believe that you have a hidden agenda, however many assurances and reassurances they have received. Start from the assumption that you are trustworthy and will be trusted. Then, if you are honest, keep your promises, and play fair with people, trust will generally follow.

LOOKING AFTER PEOPLE

Taking care of people is your prime duty as their leader. In the workplace, that involves seeing that working conditions are as pleasant as possible and that sensible requests for changes or improvements are dealt with sensitively. With individuals, it often means working as chief welfare officer. Be prepared to make exceptions to help people in trouble, and do not hesitate if you suspect problems. It is important not to allow situations to worsen. Ask if something is wrong and, if it is, act.

76 Never refuse a request without careful thought.

◀ SHOWING SYMPATHY
People bring their personal difficulties to a good leader. Whether or not the problems are affecting their work, a prompt and sympathetic response is required.

IMPARTING CONFIDENCE

Achievement builds confidence. People may doubt their ability to achieve a difficult target. When the target is met or surpassed, their feelings about themselves will improve. Reinforce these feelings by celebrating individual and team contributions, using presentations or other media. If mistakes occur, point them out, but do not undermine the person. Conscientious workers will be hard enough on themselves.

> **77** Reward success with praise as well as material recognition.

> **78** Always be loyal to your people in any public situation.

> **79** If you have to criticize someone, do so in private.

PROVIDING BACKUP

The most important support is psychological and costs nothing: loyalty. If you expect loyalty, give it. In confrontations with outsiders, support your colleagues so far as the facts will allow. Any reprimand or disciplinary action takes place in private, between leader and staff member, and not in front of third parties. Material backup is also vital. Giving people the equipment and other resources they need to perform an excellent job is no less than they deserve. Being seen to fight for resources on their behalf, moreover, will strengthen trust and loyalty.

CASE STUDY

Harry managed an important unit in which errors had reached unacceptable levels and staff morale was low. The relationship between Harry and his immediate superior, Lynn, had deteriorated to the point of non-communication. When a new functional director, George, was appointed, Lynn said that his first job was to fire Harry. But George insisted on making his own decision. He arranged a meeting at which Lynn and Harry aired their differences. They hinged around minor grievances that Lynn had failed to handle, because she took them as symptoms of Harry's general unworthiness. George dealt with the grievances, insisted that Harry and Lynn should meet only in his presence, and gave Harry his confidence. The unit's performance was transformed as Harry proved himself an excellent leader.

◀ **INSTILLING FAITH**
In this case, an important unit was performing very badly. Its leader had lost his confidence, since his immediate superior seemed to have no faith in his ability. Once the leader's confidence was restored, and his feelings about himself improved, morale and performance within his unit were quickly transformed.

ASSESSING YOUR LEADERSHIP SKILLS

Gauge your ability as an effective leader by responding to the following statements, and mark the options closest to your experience. Be as honest as you can: if your answer is "never," mark Option 1; if it is "always," mark Option 4; and so on. Add your scores together, and refer to the Analysis to see how you scored. Use your answers to identify the areas that need improving.

OPTIONS

1 Never

2 Occasionally

3 Frequently

4 Always

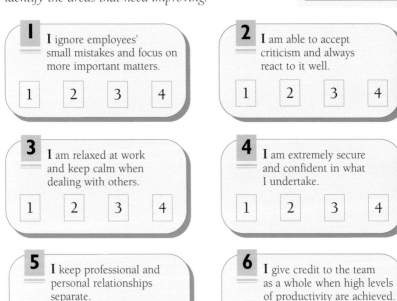

1 I ignore employees' small mistakes and focus on more important matters.

1 2 3 4

2 I am able to accept criticism and always react to it well.

1 2 3 4

3 I am relaxed at work and keep calm when dealing with others.

1 2 3 4

4 I am extremely secure and confident in what I undertake.

1 2 3 4

5 I keep professional and personal relationships separate.

1 2 3 4

6 I give credit to the team as a whole when high levels of productivity are achieved.

1 2 3 4

7 I am seen as a fair and just person who never takes sides.

| 1 | 2 | 3 | 4 |

8 I convey feelings of security and tranquillity to my team.

| 1 | 2 | 3 | 4 |

9 I convey a sense of friendliness and concern for the problems of others.

| 1 | 2 | 3 | 4 |

10 I treat people in inferior positions with respect when dealing with them.

| 1 | 2 | 3 | 4 |

11 I treat my subordinates in exactly the same way as my superiors.

| 1 | 2 | 3 | 4 |

12 I avoid making a point of being the boss, and treat others as equals.

| 1 | 2 | 3 | 4 |

13 I show that I am an excellent communicator and can motivate my team.

| 1 | 2 | 3 | 4 |

14 I participate with vigour to help my team achieve a specific goal.

| 1 | 2 | 3 | 4 |

15 I feel that I am well-respected and held in good opinion by my team.

| 1 | 2 | 3 | 4 |

16 I show impartiality in respect of colour, religion, nationality, or gender.

| 1 | 2 | 3 | 4 |

17 I accept the opinions of others, even when they differ from my own.

| 1 | 2 | 3 | 4 |

18 I am just and impartial when awarding prizes and promotions.

| 1 | 2 | 3 | 4 |

19 I endeavor to help the group stick together during a crisis.

| 1 | 2 | 3 | 4 |

20 I choose between speed and perfection, depending on the situation.

| 1 | 2 | 3 | 4 |

21 I involve myself in situations only when my intervention is required.

| 1 | 2 | 3 | 4 |

22 I demonstrate deep knowledge of my area of expertise.

| 1 | 2 | 3 | 4 |

23 I perform better than my staff if I have to replace someone temporarily.

| 1 | 2 | 3 | 4 |

24 I clearly distinguish between what is urgent and what is important.

| 1 | 2 | 3 | 4 |

25 I concentrate less on small details and give more time to important matters.

| 1 | 2 | 3 | 4 |

26 I show that I am a creative person who is always change-orientated.

| 1 | 2 | 3 | 4 |

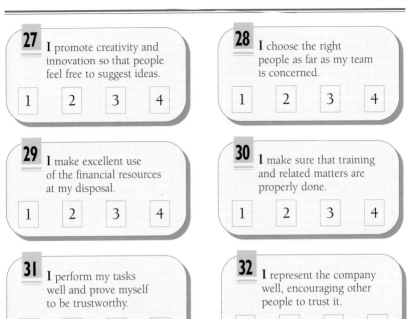

27 I promote creativity and innovation so that people feel free to suggest ideas.

1   2   3   4

28 I choose the right people as far as my team is concerned.

1   2   3   4

29 I make excellent use of the financial resources at my disposal.

1   2   3   4

30 I make sure that training and related matters are properly done.

1   2   3   4

31 I perform my tasks well and prove myself to be trustworthy.

1   2   3   4

32 I represent the company well, encouraging other people to trust it.

1   2   3   4

ANALYSIS

Now that you have completed the self-assessment, add up your total score, and check your performance by reading the corresponding evaluation. Whatever level of success you have achieved in leading people, it is important to remember that there is always room for improvement. Identify your weakest areas and refer to the relevant chapters to find practical advice to help you develop and refine your leadership skills.

32–64: You may be losing the authority to lead. Use this opportunity to learn from your mistakes and improve your performance, using this book to help you.
65–95: Your leadership skills are generally sound but could improve. Develop those areas where you scored poorly.
96–128: You are a fine leader. Now work to improve further.

INSPIRING EXCELLENCE

The difference between leadership and management lies in the leader's ability to inspire the will to excel. Spur people on to achieve their best through motivation and example.

MOTIVATING OTHERS

People are capable of remarkable achievement if they are given the right motivational leadership. To mobilize a team's inner drive, enthusiasm, and vigor effectively, you need to be a credible leader who sets an inspiring example.

80 Never seek to get results by bullying people beneath you.

81 Use discipline sparingly, but make it swift and effective.

82 Keep the "carrot" visible but the "stick" in hiding.

SHARING A PURPOSE

The key to motivation is to communicate a strong sense of shared purpose. That can only be developed, of course, by sharing the purpose, involving everybody in plans, reviews, and getting results. Organize regular meetings to ensure that staff are up-to-date on the progress of the company. This knowledge makes team members more aware of their roles. As a result, they feel that their efforts make a difference to achieving common goals. Create the desire to succeed, not only for personal gratification, but also out of a sense of identification with the team objective.

SETTING AN EXAMPLE

A decisive leader who welcomes change and shows personal drive develops similar qualities in others. People will strive to excel for a leader in whose strength and wisdom they truly believe. Your own standards are therefore crucial. On top of that foundation, a high level of energy and purposeful activity is vital.

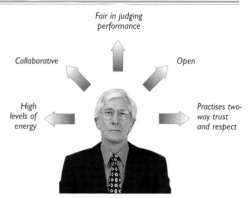

Fair in judging performance

Collaborative

Open

High levels of energy

Practises two-way trust and respect

▲ EVALUATING THE INSPIRATIONAL LEADER

A leader must be fair, open, trustworthy, and wise to inspire others. He or she also needs boundless energy and enthusiasm. Without these qualities, the basis for credibility will not exist.

TESTING YOUR CREDIBILITY

If you can agree with the statements below, you are a credible leader who is able to inspire others.

- I perform to the highest level of competence.
- I take initiatives and risks.
- I adapt to change.
- I make decisions promptly.
- I work cooperatively as a team member.
- I am open, especially with information and knowledge.
- I trust and am trustworthy.
- I respect others and myself.
- I answer for my actions and accept responsibility.
- I judge and am judged, reward and am rewarded, on the basis of performance.

KEEPING MOTIVATION HIGH

When problems or failures occur, a good leader confronts them squarely and seeks to understand their causes before using them as springboards for success. After a careful analysis of the reasons behind failure, be prepared to take responsibility for your own errors. Making honest mistakes once is common and is forgivable in a motivating, no-blame culture. But to keep motivation high, you cannot allow mistakes to be repeated time and again. Discuss with your staff what can be learned from these expensive lessons, and ensure that they are equipped to do better next time.

83 Share responsibility for mistakes and failures, and analyze errors so you can prevent them next time.

ESTABLISHING A VISION

Human beings find it easier to look back rather than forward. But effective and inspirational leadership begins with the long view. Establish a vision of where you want to be in the long term, and your visionary zeal will inspire others to look to the future.

84 Write down your ambitions, and revise them periodically.

DEVELOPING A VISION

85 If your vision seems unattainable, simply intensify your efforts.

A vision is an aim for the future – at any level, from team, to department, to organization. To develop a vision, define what you are aiming to achieve in the future, and compare it with where you are now. Map out what you will need to bridge the gap, from extra staff or training to purchasing new technology. As leader, you must consider all the necessary steps to achieve the vision.

RECOGNIZING ATTITUDES

VISIONARY
Can see the benefits of change, and has the courage to carry out change despite obstacles.

PRAGMATIST
Will accept innovation, but only after it has been proved to work by somebody else.

CONSERVATIVE
Resists change and is creative only in inventing excuses for rejecting the new.

CREATING VISIONARIES

Any organization can be broken down into visionaries, pragmatists, and conservatives. The last group leads the opposition to change, while pragmatists are followers rather than leaders. You need the pragmatist's interest in proof, facts, and figures and the conservative's attachment to abiding values and accumulated experience. But both need to be animated by the visionary's strong leadership. Involving pragmatists and conservatives in plans for change may, over time, make them more ready to share visions.

EXPRESSING A VISION

Visions need to be expressed as statements to communicate a clear understanding of the long-term aim and the principles underlying it. When creating such a statement, ask yourself if anybody reading it would be able to extract a practical understanding of the business you are in, where your leadership is going, and how it is getting there. That requires a triple focus: on the customers, on the people who serve the customers, and on the constantly improved performance that makes that service excellent. Ensure that you apply that focus in ways that are different to and better than the competition. That is unlikely to be the case if your statement reads much like everybody else's. Become the strongest critic of your own vision.

86 Keep vision and mission wording brief, clear, and prescriptive.

87 Give statements to others to check before you finalize them.

STRENGTHENING VISION STATEMENTS

WEAK STATEMENTS	QUESTIONS RAISED	STRONG STATEMENTS
"We have a strong people orientation and demonstrate care for every employee in the company."	● What does "people orientation" mean in practice? ● What kind of "care?"	"We will lead local suppliers in share, product/service quality, value, customer satisfaction, and good conduct by being different and measurably better."
"We sustain a strong results orientation coupled with a prudent approach to business."	● What does "results orientation" mean in practice? ● What is "prudence" about?	"Strategies, policies, and implementation are designed for and by our people, who ally with suppliers to achieve high customer ratings."
"Our aim is to be the biggest and best in our market."	● What do "biggest and best" actually mean? ● On what criteria are they applied?	"We invest and innovate to double real revenues every three years, while raising operating profits, cash flow, giving added value, and sharing the rewards."

GENERATING IDEAS

The leader does not have to be the most inventive person on the team. But as leader, you need to release the potential for generating ideas that exists in all individuals and teams. This will help in both achieving a vision and resolving day-to-day issues.

88 Make people see that it is everyone's job to generate ideas.

PROMOTING CREATIVITY

Actively promote creativity by example, encouragement, rewards, training, procedures, budgeting processes, and promotion. Lower any creative barriers by tolerating failure and eccentricity, flattening organizational structures and removing blockages, and refusing to tolerate concepts such as "Not invented here," "It will never work," "If it was any good somebody else would have done it," and their equivalents. Also, recognize that consensus can be the enemy of creativity, and do not allow the pursuit of agreement to kill creative initiatives. If a creative idea is proposed to you, always consider it.

89 Try to implement suggestions, as long as they will cause no harm.

STIMULATING IDEAS

If you wait for ideas to come, they probably will not. A few rare people spout ideas all the time. But most of those attending an ideas meeting will be relatively quiet participants. To stop that from happening, insist on two rules. First, everybody must come to the meeting with two or three genuinely new ideas, which can be as far-fetched as they like. Second, nobody is allowed to "shoot ideas down in flames" – trashing proposals without discussion. The important needs are to get ideas on the table and to encourage everybody to believe in their own powers of idea generation.

Challenger visualizes an idea

Dreamer conceptualizes the idea

BRAINSTORMING

Getting people together to generate ideas, or brainstorming, has sent many groups down the wrong path to creativity. Badly practiced, it encourages the belief that throwing ideas into the pot is itself creative. Organized creativity is far more effective. A simple procedure is to start by analyzing the situation and to end with a shortlist of strong ideas. At each stage of this process there should be a challenging session, in which people can challenge assumptions. Often what is taken for granted should not be.

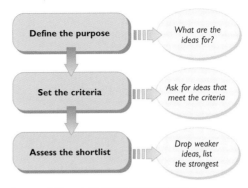

Define the purpose → What are the ideas for?

Set the criteria → Ask for ideas that meet the criteria

Assess the shortlist → Drop weaker ideas, list the strongest

▲ IDENTIFYING THE BEST IDEAS

Organized creativity can be extremely productive.
A brainstorming meeting should be divided into three main stages, enabling the group to agree on a shortlist of strong ideas.

Explorer analyzes the idea

Map maker mobilizes troops and resources

Path cutter realizes the idea and makes it happen

90 Make sure ideas are challenged with respect and not with contempt.

◀ UNDERSTANDING INNOVATION

A good creative team comprises individuals who can take an idea from conception to fruition. The first stage is to come up with a concept. Next, the team must assess whether the concept will work, evaluate the practical implications, and decide how the idea will be implemented. Finally, the plan has to be followed through. Each stage fits and needs different personalities.

MANAGING OPENLY

Sharing information has a positive effect on performance. Withholding it has the opposite effect. By trusting your staff with information and by being open and honest with them, you will help and inspire them to perform better.

91 If unsure about whether or not you should pass on information, do so.

COMMUNICATING FULLY

As the leader of a multinational company said, "However much you communicate, it is never enough." Information is the lifeblood of an organization, and communication its main artery. Make sure that the channels of communication are always open in all directions. Keeping staff up-to-date with the latest developments generates goodwill toward the company. Use every means available to ensure that whatever you know, your staff know, and as soon as possible.

Leader openly discusses facts and figures with team member

SECRETIVE MANAGEMENT

Employee acts deceptively to gain information

AVOIDING SECRECY ▲

Unnecessary secrecy demoralizes people and diminishes their potential. Conversely, their performance is enhanced, often greatly, by fuller knowledge. Financial information, for instance, is often on the secret list. But if people are given figures that reflect the performance of their part of the company, they will understand the financial results of their actions.

OPEN MANAGEMENT

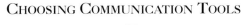

CHOOSING COMMUNICATION TOOLS

E-MAIL
This prime means of communication is fast, effective, and user-friendly.

MEETINGS
Face-to-face meetings build relationships and trust, and promote instant feedback.

JOURNALISM
In-house newsletters and magazines are a good way of keeping people informed.

INTERNAL MARKETING
Colorful marketing is a good way of "selling" change using consumer techniques.

NOTICEBOARDS
Bulletin boards are a basic means of giving information that can also be used by staff.

TELEPHONE
The telephone is vital for one-on-one communication, but not for lengthy talks.

SHARING INFORMATION

Open management involves regular exchanges of information between leaders and team members. Problems and tactics are discussed openly, and everybody is invited to make suggestions. Open management favors the creation of a positive, motivational atmosphere in the workplace: staff feel that they are part of the decision process and that their opinions are valued. Leaders also benefit: they can keep a finger on the pulse and learn of potential problems at an early stage. Make sure that you are visible and approachable: staying behind closed doors makes you remote and inaccessible. Be available for discussion and, if you can, facilitate collaboration among team members by having open-plan layouts.

92 Ensure that your messages reach all members of staff.

93 Make sure that you encourage staff to participate in decision-making.

BOOSTING ACHIEVEMENT

A good leader insists on positive outcomes for both short-term goals and for the long-term vision. Make sure that team members know what your desired result is, and monitor their performance as individuals and as a team in terms of output.

---

94 Always keep your mind firmly on the outcome that you are seeking.

---

95 Encourage people to seek clarification if they are unsure about any of their objectives.

CHOOSING A MONITORING SYSTEM

SYSTEM	RESULT
WRITTEN REPORTS Staff provide written summary of actions, results, and figures.	Encourages staff to organize their thoughts and review their actions clearly.
PERSONAL REPORTS Regular meetings are held with each team member to assess progress.	Allows for informal updates and facilitates early airings of potential problems.
OPEN-DOOR POLICY Individuals are encouraged to discuss day-to-day problems at any time.	Shows strong support, but may prevent team members from using their initiative.
APPRAISAL Formal interviews are held to assess performance and set improvement targets.	Appraisal produces improved results if practiced continuously and informally.

MONITORING PROGRESS

It is essential to keep an eye on how plans are progressing so that you can spot problems early. If all is going well, you may want to raise targets to exploit the opportunity. The key is to make progress measurable. For example, build in key dates and quality targets, and compare budgets with actual expenditure. Regular checks should help you and your staff to adjust targets, budgets, and so on, while keeping teams on course to achieve the desired outcome. As a leader, you are in a good position to see the overall picture – if several aspects are going awry, drastic action may be needed.

---

96 Make the outcome measurable if at all possible.

JUDGING OUTPUT

Are your staff contributing enough towards the overall desired outcome? If the answer is "Yes," your leadership has passed the first and most important test. If the reply is "No," you have two options. Either tell subordinates precisely what you want from them and how you want it achieved, or be clear about the outcome and leave the choice of route and methods to them.

97 Get staff fully involved in achieving the ultimate objective.

98 Let your staff know exactly what you expect from them.

99 Use appraisals to develop your staff, not as ends in themselves.

RAISING OUTPUT

Annual appraisals provide an opportunity for a leader to discuss performance and output with staff and to set targets for improvement. However, you will find the process far easier if you practice continuous appraisal, talking to everyone about their jobs. This informal contact helps to keep people focused on desired outcomes, as well as keeping you up to date with their progress. Provide feedback to ensure that staff feel a sense of direction and achievement; ask for and act on their input; and provide support and training readily when necessary. Continuous involvement should help to boost morale and raise output.

HELPING PEOPLE TO IMPROVE OUTPUT

It is important to talk to people regularly about their jobs and how you and they think performance could be improved. Remember to include your own role in the discussion. Always use positive questions, such as the following:

Is there anything you think could be done better?

What am I doing that is stopping you from performing your job better?

Can I do something that would help you to excel?

Is there any way in which we could change the project to achieve better results?

BEING COMPETITIVE

*E*ntrepreneurs, people who spot and take a new business opportunity, are inspirational leaders who know that it is vital to accept the risk of failure to achieve anything worthwhile. Emulate such people by seeing risks and threats as opportunities.

> **100** Do not gamble, but back your own best judgment in going for results.

IDENTIFYING OPPORTUNITIES

Taking charge of a project may not in itself be entrepreneurial, but you still need to identify and express the objective, form and activate an effective team, and realize the ultimate goal by executing an excellent plan. The more you behave like an entrepreneur, the more successful your leadership is likely to be. What opportunities exist – not only in the marketplace, but internally – that could bring higher profits and greater customer satisfaction? What new, higher ambitions will transform the unit's prospects?

TAKING RISKS

Leaders realize that every opportunity involves two risks: first, that the perceived opportunity may not exist; second, if it does, that poor execution may lose you the perceived chance. Either way, the resulting failure can cause loss and humiliation. But the key to risk-taking is certainty: you must have complete confidence in your ability to win. You should also take every care (using analytical and intuitive skills) to ensure that you do not lose. Do this by listing the possible consequences of the risk, and assess how likely each is to occur. Be clear-sighted, and seek to minimize negative consequences and maximize positive ones.

The chance of making gains is small

The risk of large losses is great

▲ WEIGHING UP THE RISK

It makes no sense to risk large losses (the downside) in order to make small gains (the upside). Always compare the downside risk with the upside potential to make sure that the risk is really worthwhile. If not, you need to look at ways of substantially reducing the risk or increasing the gains.

TACKLING COMPETITION

All leaders want to outdo the competition. As well as a spirit of determination, this takes careful thought and forward planning. Do not base your actions or reactions on the belief that a rival business is bound to fail or does not know what it is doing. Instead, assume that the competition will succeed unless you mount a vigorous response. Never ignore signs that customers prefer other, competitive offerings. The true competitor must outperform rivals on every aspect that matters to the customer.

POINTS TO REMEMBER

- Reports and rumors of errors by opponents should never lead you to lower your guard.
- Reports of opponents' successes should not be discounted either.
- All angles and alternatives should be considered before reacting.
- Respond to a threat with a better strategy that turns the tables on the competition.

101 Keep up-to-date on the progress of competitors.

COVERING EVERY ANGLE

Leaders must always be on the lookout for potential threats. The main questions to ask are:

COMPETITION AND THE MARKET
- Could newcomers create damaging competition?
- Is there an existing powerful force in the market that could muscle into your territory?
- Does a competitor have a stronger hold on your biggest customers?
- Is the market developing in ways that favor competitors more than you?
- Is there a growing market segment where you are being left behind?

CUSTOMERS
- Are you aware of the latest customer feedback?
- Could your customers take away major sources of revenue?

OUTSIDE THREATS
- Is there a rival technology or other development that could generate a major difference?
- Could an unsuspected challenge arrive from outside the existing industry?

PLAYING TO WIN

Running scared is much healthier than being overly complacent. To avoid complacency, always analyze your strengths, weaknesses, opportunities, and threats, and those of the competition. Keep abreast of changes and developments in your field, and spend time analyzing trends. Some threats can be predicted, but unpredictable threats increasingly arise. With a flexible attitude, you will be ready to treat each one on its merits.

INDEX

ACKNOWLEDGMENTS

AUTHOR'S ACKNOWLEDGMENTS

This book owes its existence to the perceptive inspiration of Stephanie Jackson and Nigel Duffield at Dorling Kindersley; and I owe more than I can say to the expertise and enthusiasm of Jane Simmonds and all the editorial and design staff who worked on the project. I am also greatly indebted to the many colleagues, friends, and other management luminaries on whose wisdom and information I have drawn.

PUBLISHER'S ACKNOWLEDGMENTS

DK Publishing would like to thank the following for their help and participation in producing this book:

Editorial Alison Bolus, Michael Downey, Nicola Munro, Jane Simmonds, Sylvia Tombesi-Walton; **Design** Pauline Clarke, Jamie Hanson, Nigel Morris, Tish Mills; **DTP assistance** Rob Campbell; **Indexer** Hilary Bird.

Photography Steve Gorton; **Photography assistance** Nick Harper, Andy Komorowski.

Models Phil Argent, Richard Hill, Cornell John, Janey Madlani, Karen Murray, Peter Taylor, Suki Tan.

Makeup Debbie Finlow, Janice Tee.

Suppliers Geiger Brickel (Office Furniture), Bally (Shoes). With thanks to Tony Ash at Geiger Brickel and Carron Williams at Bally.

Picture research Andy Sansom; **Picture library assistance** Sue Hadley, Rachel Hilford, Denise O'Brien, Melanie Simmonds.

PICTURE CREDITS

Key: *a* above, *b* bottom, *c* centre, *l* left, *r* right, *t* top
NASA 40*b*; **Telegraph Colour Library** Benelux Press 47*tr*, Larry Bray 43*l*, Ryanstock 4, front jacket *tl*.

AUTHOR'S BIOGRAPHY

Robert Heller is a leading authority in the world of management consulting and was the founding editor of Britain's top management magazine, *Management Today*. He is much in demand as a conference speaker in Europe, North and South America, and the Far East. As editorial director of Haymarket Publishing Group, Robert Heller supervised the launch of several highly successful magazines such as *Campaign*, *Computing*, and *Accountancy Age*. His many acclaimed – and worldwide bestselling – books include *The Naked Manager*, *Culture Shock*, *The Age of the Common Millionaire*, *The Way to Win* (with Will Carling), *The Complete Guide to Modern Management*, and *In Search of European Excellence*. Robert Heller has also written a number of earlier books in the DK Publishing *Essential Managers* series.